D

PAINTING

by
Colin Caket

Piccolo
A Piper Book

Contents

Introduction

In the heart of the Sahara Desert, where no plant or grazing animal now survives, an ancient artist once scratched the image of a pair of antelope on an overhanging rock (shown above). In 1970, I climbed a wall of blistering rock and rediscovered these engravings. After nine thousand years they still looked fresh and alive – because the long-forgotten artist knew exactly what he was doing!

His tools may have been crude, but he knew how to handle them. And he knew his subject as well as he knew his materials. He observed antelope every day, studying their habits and hunting them. So when he came to scratch their image onto hard rock, he knew just which features to choose.

Learning to look

Since the days of that Stone Age artist, mankind has built the Pyramids, evolved writing from pictures, and walked on the Moon. We now have a wider choice of subjects, and a wider range of materials to draw or paint them with. But we still need to understand the materials we use. We still draw best what we know best. We still have to decide what to put in and what to leave out of our pictures.

You can't paint *every* leaf on a tree, for example, so you have to look for the way leaves group themselves into masses, and paint these masses rather than each leaf.

The art of every culture is now available for us to study in books. New ideas crowd at us from posters, magazines and television, so we tend to measure ourselves against expert, professional artists instead of the chap painting the cave next door! But remember that you usually see only an artist's best work. He probably

▶ A mural based on Blake's poem, *Tiger Tiger*, with the artists.

4

▲ Portrait by Tana Meinertz-hagen (reproduced half size).

just copying the Japanese way of portraying nature, they were inspired to take a fresh look at nature themselves.

It is a mistake to copy other people's paintings, but I don't know a single artist who doesn't use photographs for reference. It is sometimes said that copying is cheating, but copying photographs is cheating only if you make no effort to understand and learn from what you are doing. If you don't try to learn you are certainly cheating yourself!

had several goes at it before he got it right, so don't worry if you need to have several goes too.

Drawings and paintings in books are almost always reduced in size. Don't be tricked by this into working on too small a scale. The pictures in this book are, wherever possible, reproduced at the size they were drawn or painted. If not, the size of the original is given, so try to make allowances for this.

Learning from others

There is always something to learn from the way other artists tackle problems. For example, the group of artists known as the French Impressionists were inspired by woodcut prints from Japan, which came to France as wrapping paper. But instead of

Tools and materials

A camera is just another tool for the artist to use, like a pen or a rubber. You sometimes hear it said that using a rubber is cheating too. This is rubbish, but you *do* need to learn to get the best out of a rubber, just as you have to learn to use a pencil or a paintbrush or any other type of tool.

There is a far wider range of artists' materials available than it is possible to cover in this book, so I have listed the most useful to start with, and given some suggestions on how to use them.

The materials you use don't have to be expensive or complicated. But materials bought from artists' suppliers are specially designed for drawing or painting, and the assistant who sells them should be able to advise you how to use them. Your art teacher will advise you too, but your *best* teacher is yourself. Learning through trial, error and experiment is what makes it fun!

Experimenting

It is always exciting to try new materials and find out what you can do with them. I knew an artist in Nigeria who worked in silver. His products were naturally not very big. Then sheet aluminium was introduced into the area as roofing material. He discovered that, if polished, aluminium is as bright as silver. So he worked with aluminium instead, banging it up from the back to turn the sheets into huge, gleaming panels that were much more exciting than his earlier work.

The scale he was able to work on was what made the difference between silver and aluminium for him. The differences *you* find between the materials you try may have nothing to do with scale, but every material you use will have new possibilities which might make a big difference to your work.

But don't be too eager to try something new just because what you are using doesn't work. It could be because you haven't learned to *make* it work. If you can't draw with a pencil, for example, it is unlikely that you will be able to draw with anything else!

▼ A decorative aluminium panel made by a Yoruba artist, Asiru Olatunde. (Detail shown 25cm × 35cm.)

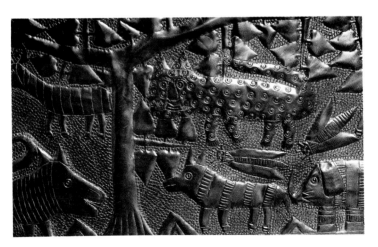

1: Choosing and Using Drawing Materials

To get the most out of your materials you need to know their strengths and their weaknesses.

With pen and ink, for example, you get a lovely clean line – but that's *all* you get! If you want to use **shading** in a pen drawing you have to make it up from a series of lines. With chalks you can get a range of **shades**, and you can tone one shade into another, but you can't get as clean a line as you can with a pen.

Every new material has different possibilities. It's no good trying to force materials to do things they can't do, although you sometimes have to try to do this, just to find out what they *can* do!

Paper

Any unlined paper without a shiny surface is good for drawing on. *Layout pads* are relatively cheap to buy and, because

layout paper is also semi-transparent, you can tear off a first attempt at a drawing and put it under the next sheet as a guide for another attempt.

You can draw in pencil, chalks and most types of ink on layout paper, but DON'T USE INDIAN INK. This sort of ink shrinks as it dries and pulls the thin layout paper into wrinkles. *Cartridge* paper is better for Indian ink drawing, and is the best quality paper you are likely to need at first. Cartridge paper can be bought as single sheets or in pads.

Pencils

Pencils are graded according to the hardness or softness of their lead. The softer the lead, the blacker the mark it makes on paper. Soft pencils have a **B** (for black) on the side, and hard pencils have an **H**. They also have a number before the letter. The higher the number in front

Harder ⟵⟵ **Softer** ⟶

| 6H | 5H | 4H | 3H | 2H | H | HB | B | 2B | 3B | 4B | 5B | 6B |

8

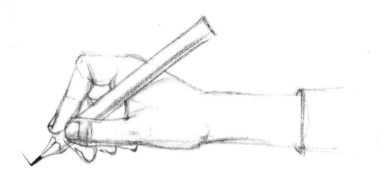

▲ Draw with the point of the lead . . .

▲ . . . and with the side of the lead too.

of the **H**, the *harder* the lead. The higher the number in front of the **B**, the *softer* the lead. Soft pencils, from about **2B** to **6B**, are usually best for drawing.

DON'T sharpen the end with the letter and number on it, then you will be able to see which pencil you want, however short it gets.

Never use a blunt pencil, and try to use the *side* of the lead to draw with, as well as the point. To do this you have to hold the pencil flatter onto the paper.

under your hand between your thumb and four fingers.

Practise by making several drawings using *only* the side of the lead. Try to concentrate less on outlines and more on whole areas of light or dark tones. Soon you should be able to draw equally well with the side or with the point of the lead, using the side for shading and the point for lines and details.

Never try to get darker tones just by pressing harder. You *do* have to press a little harder, of

▲ Drawing made with the point of the lead.

▶ Drawing made with the side of the lead.

course, but pressing too hard will destroy the surface of the paper. It is better to build up the darker parts of your drawing by going over them several times.

Charcoal

Pencil lead isn't lead at all, but graphite – which is a type of carbon. Charcoal is a softer sort of carbon, made by burning sticks of wood in a special way.

Drawing with charcoal sticks gives rich black tones, which can be removed from the paper more easily than pencil lead. Use a *putty rubber* to remove it, or the soft, moist bread from inside a white loaf.

Charcoal is so easy to remove that you can work more into your drawings, softening dark

▲ Charcoal portrait drawn by Tana Meinertz-hagen (half size).

areas with a finger and making **highlights** with a putty rubber squeezed to a point. But nothing is easier to smudge accidentally than charcoal, so you will need to *fix* your drawings. (See the end of this chapter for the section on fixative.)

Rubbers

Some people say that you shouldn't use a rubber when drawing. This is rubbish. But it *is* better to let your mistakes accumulate, then deal with them all together.

It is easier to draw accurately if you lightly sketch in the broad **structure** of your subject first, then add more detail to this **framework**. These guidelines can be rubbed out when the drawing is finished, if necessary.

Soft *India rubbers* are best for erasing pencil. The surface of the rubber should be rubbed away, *not* the surface of the paper! Clean your rubber on a spare bit of paper before you use it. If you only want to erase a small detail, slice off a piece of the rubber to get a sharp edge.

Hold the paper flat with one hand with your thumb and fingers separated, and use the rubber between them. This way you won't crease the paper. If necessary, protect the parts of your drawing that you *don't* want erased by putting a piece of paper under your fingers and thumb.

▲ Using a rubber.

Sometimes you need to use a rubber to soften a line, rather than to erase it completely, or to lighten an area you have made too dark. The best rubber for this is a *plastic* or putty rubber, which can be squeezed to a point and won't smudge your drawing. Putty rubbers are also ideal for using with chalk, as well as with charcoal.

Pen and ink

Many different kinds of pen are available. The more traditional type have a replaceable split-metal nib that has to be dipped in ink. Some modern pens have a built-in supply of ink. *Ball-point* pens are usually not much good for drawing with because the ink tends to blob. *Felt-* and *fibre-tipped* pens are better. Those with spirit-based inks (rather than water-based) dry almost instantly, so there is little danger of smudging your drawing.

Felt tips come in a range of colours, but you can only mix the colours by using one on top of another. You can't run one colour into another as you can with paints or chalks.

All pens basically do the same thing – they draw a line. If you want to add shading to a pen drawing, you have to make it up from a series or more or less **parallel** lines called *hatching*. A second series of parallel lines,

▲ Drawing made with coloured felt-tipped pens.

▲ Outlines with some shading.

drawn at an angle across the first lot, is called *cross-hatching.*

Practise hatching until you can get the lines fairly straight and evenly spaced. When you can do this, draw a simple object (an apple, for example) by outlining the dark, medium and light areas and filling up the shapes you have drawn with hatching and cross-hatching. Then make a similar drawing, but this time without an outline to guide you. Finally, try another drawing without worrying too much about trying to keep the lines straight.

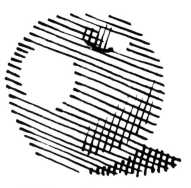

▲ Shading with no outlines.

Chalks

It is best to use artists' chalks, which are designed for drawing on paper and come in a wide range of colours. Use the side of a stick of chalk to cover large areas and the tip for more detailed drawing.

▲ A livelier and more free style of pen and ink drawing.

▼ These drawings were done using three shades of grey chalk.

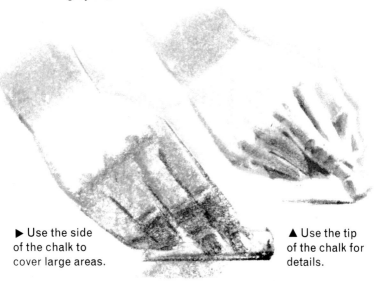

▶ Use the side of the chalk to cover large areas.

▲ Use the tip of the chalk for details.

Mix the colours by drawing one on top of another, and smudge them together with your fingertip. Work out which areas you want to remain light before you have gone too far. DON'T try to use a light chalk over a darker one. The darker colour will show through, especially when you fix it.

Chalk drawings have to be fixed when finished to stop them getting smudged accidentally. So draw in the lighter areas last, or go over them again in the same colour before you fix them. Otherwise, any tiny specks of darker chalk that

have fallen onto the lighter parts can spread to become blobs when drenched with a fixative spray.

With charcoal or pencil drawings you build up the dark areas by going over them again and again until you have the right **depth** of shading, and for lighter areas you simply use less shading. You can do this with chalk drawings too, of course, but with chalks you can *also* buy different shades of grey or coloured chalk to get the exact tone you want. There are often many shades available, but three shades – light, medium and dark – are usually enough. You can smudge them together with your fingertip to get **intermediate** shades.

Fixative

There are several makes of clear fixative available, most of them in aerosol cans. The cans have clear instructions printed on them, which you should follow.

In general, you should not spray the fixative too close to the drawing, or spray so much onto it that the liquid runs on the surface. AVOID BREATHING THE FUMES, AND NEVER SPRAY THE FIXATIVE NEAR A FLAME OR THROW THE USED CAN ONTO A FIRE.

▲ Coloured chalk drawing (27cm × 25cm).

2: Proportion

Getting the proportion right in drawing means measuring, by eye, the various sizes, shapes and positions of the different parts of your subject.

We all have a reasonably good sense of what is **vertical** and what is **horizontal**. If we didn't, we'd fall over! It is this sense you have to use. Look for features which are directly one above another, or on the same horizontal line. Lightly draw in these features first, and use them as reference points for the rest of your drawing.

Copying from flat originals

Judging proportion needs practice. Start with something flat

and two-dimensional, rather than a solid object.

Copy illustrations from old newspapers and magazines. Choose something simple and uncluttered. Cartoons are ideal, but any picture with a clear outline will do.

Grid patterns
It is easier at first *not* to trust your eye alone, but to use a *grid pattern* to help you.

Draw a grid pattern of squares onto the picture you want to copy. This gives you a number of points of reference where the lines of the grid cross the lines of the picture.

Draw another grid with the same number and size of squares onto a separate sheet of paper. Lightly mark the reference points on this other grid and use them as a guide for your copying.

Scaling up or down
When you have made a few accurate copies using a grid

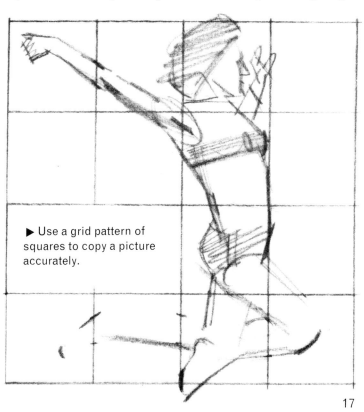

▶ Use a grid pattern of squares to copy a picture accurately.

17

pattern, try *scaling up* a picture. Make the grid of squares on your paper larger than those on the picture. Mark the points of reference on the larger grid, allowing for the increased size of the squares. Use them as a guide for your finished copy.

You can scale pictures *down* in size too, of course, by making the squares on your paper *smaller* than those on the original picture. Or try making a copy face the other way to the original. This is called 'reversing left

▼ Scale up a picture by using larger squares on your copy.

to right', and it isn't quite so straightforward!

Measuring by eye

Once you can do all this with confidence, choose another picture and try to copy it accurately without using a grid. Look for horizontal and vertical relationships and mark them lightly in pencil on paper. Now look for those features that are *not* related vertically or horizontally and try to judge the angle between them. Lightly mark these in too, then mark in key features, such as a person's eyes or elbows.

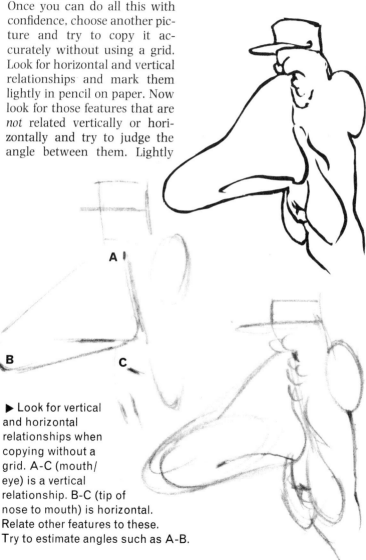

▶ Look for vertical and horizontal relationships when copying without a grid. A-C (mouth/eye) is a vertical relationship. B-C (tip of nose to mouth) is horizontal. Relate other features to these. Try to estimate angles such as A-B.

When you have got all the reference points down accurately use them as the basis for more detailed drawing.

Also try to make a copy which is larger or smaller than the original, without a grid pattern to keep the parts properly in proportion. Try reversing a picture left to right too, if you like puzzles!

▲ Copy drawings or photographs to a larger scale, trying to keep the larger drawing in proportion to the original.

Drawing solid objects

Now try 'copying' a solid, three-dimensional object instead of a flat picture. This is more difficult because the slightest change of position changes the shape you are looking at!

Choose something fairly small and simple to start with – a toy or an ornament, for example. First mark in the key points as before, using them as the basis for the rest of your drawing. Draw very lightly at first, sketching in the broad shapes. Add darker tones and details when you are satisfied that the overall proportions are correct.

▶ Three stages in drawing.
(1) Key points, vertical and horizontal relationships.
(2) The basic structure.
(3) Detail and shading added.

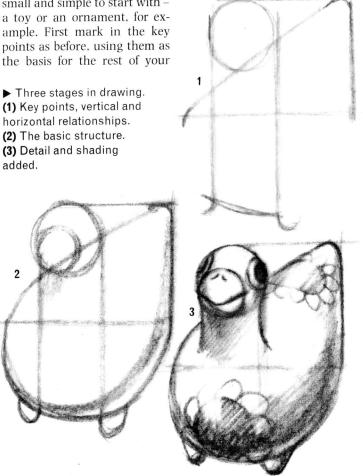

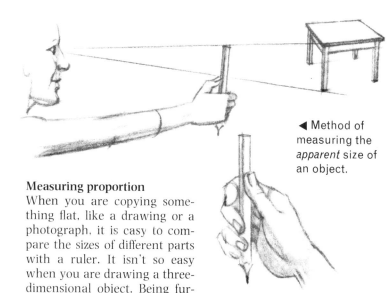

◀ Method of measuring the *apparent* size of an object.

Measuring proportion

When you are copying something flat, like a drawing or a photograph, it is easy to compare the sizes of different parts with a ruler. It isn't so easy when you are drawing a three-dimensional object. Being further away, or at a different angle, affects the *apparent* shape or size of the different parts.

For example, the more distant leg of a table is the same length as the nearer leg, but it *looks* shorter because it is further away. It is the *apparent* length you need to measure when drawing, not the actual length. You can't measure the apparent length with a ruler, but you *can* measure it with a pencil!

Close all four fingers of one hand round one end of the pencil. Hold it vertically towards your subject with your arm straight. Close one eye and line up the top of the pencil with the top of the object to be measured.

Hold it quite steady and slide your thumbnail up the side of the pencil. Stop when it lines up with the bottom of whatever you are measuring. Keep your thumbnail in position and move your arm, keeping it straight, to compare this dimension with others. Turn your hand to a horizontal position to compare width with height, and so on.

As you become more practised, learn to judge proportion by eye alone. Sometimes you might not have time to make accurate measurements.

Animals, for example, rarely keep still for long, and might disappear over the horizon at any moment. So try to draw quickly and confidently, *feeling* for big, broad shapes with light strokes of your pencil. Ignore the details until you have got the basic framework right, then build a more finished drawing onto this framework. Don't start on the details until you have a framework to relate them to.

Recording proportions

Different readers using this book will want to draw different

▲ Sketch in a framework first.

▶ Then add details and shading to your drawing.

things. It would be impossible to list the proportions of everything everyone might want to draw! So try to notice the proportions of different things and measure and record them yourself.

Remember that individual objects usually conform to a general pattern. Individual makes of car, for example, are built in more or less the same way, but vary in the proportion of their parts. Many animals, too, are built in the same way – but vary enormously in the proportion of their different parts. A mouse is constructed along the same lines as an elephant, but its shape is very different. Your skeleton is identical to the skeleton of a frog – except that the proportions are different. Once you understand the general rule it is easier to make sense of individual differences.

▶ An adult is about 7 heads tall. A four-year-old is about 5 heads tall. A newborn baby's head is about a third of the length of its body.

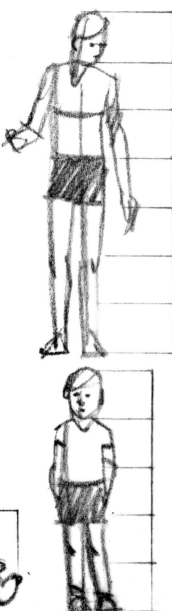

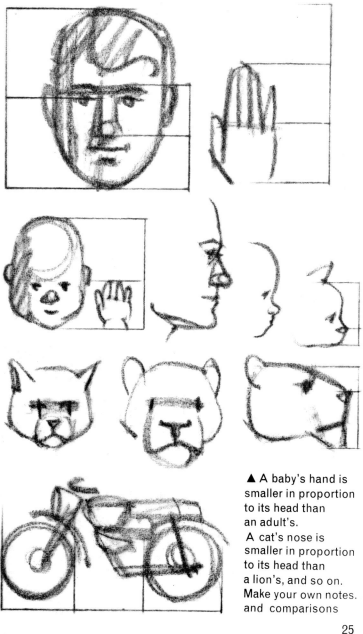

▲ A baby's hand is
smaller in proportion
to its head than
an adult's.
A cat's nose is
smaller in proportion
to its head than
a lion's, and so on.
Make your own notes.
and comparisons

25

3: Perspective

Perspective is used in drawing and painting to help create a sense of depth and space.

The best known effect of perspective is that objects which are further off look smaller. But things which are very distant also look fainter and more blue in colour.

Aerial perspective

Far away objects look fainter because you are looking at them through a thicker layer of

air. Air isn't perfectly transparent and fine details disappear over a distance, leaving just big, flat shapes.

Because *blue* light travels through air more easily than other colours, distant things also look blue. This effect is called aerial perspective and you can use it to suggest distance in landscape paintings.

Vanishing points

When things are further away they look smaller. You can see this effect of perspective very clearly with walls and roads, which have parallel sides.

The parallel sides of a wall or a road seem to get closer together as they recede into the distance. If the road is very long and straight, the sides will appear to meet in the distance.

The point where they appear to meet is called the *vanishing point*. With a wall or a house, the parallel sides usually end before they appear to meet. You have to extend them in your imagination (or lightly with a pencil, if you are drawing) to find the vanishing point (1).

When the parallel lines are horizontal, as the tops and bottoms of walls usually are, the vanishing point will be on the horizon. But not *all* vanishing points are on the horizon – you only have to stand close to a tall building and look up to prove that (2)!

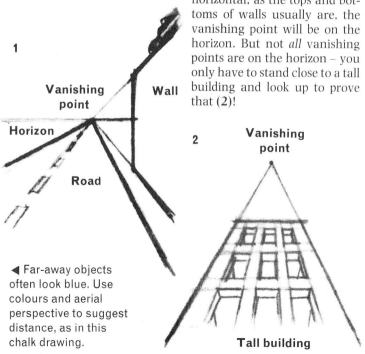

1

Vanishing point

Wall

Horizon

Road

◀ Far-away objects often look blue. Use colours and aerial perspective to suggest distance, as in this chalk drawing.

2

Vanishing point

Tall building

If you look at a house from an angle, so that two of its sides are visible at once, each side will have its own vanishing point. If the top and bottom of each wall are horizontal both vanishing points will be on the horizon (1). The tops and bottoms of windows and doors are usually horizontal too, so lines drawn from these to the horizon should all meet at the same vanishing point as the walls they are on (2).

Try drawing something quite complicated, like a castle, with towers, walls and battlements. All the parallel lines for each side should meet at the same vanishing points (3).

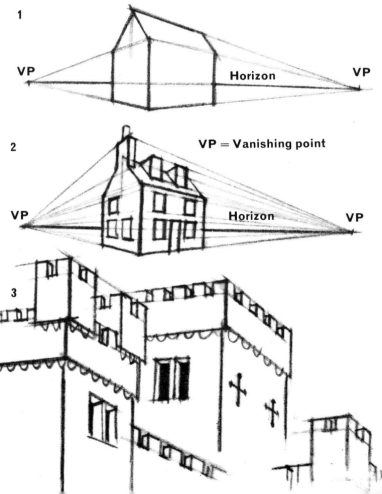

1

VP Horizon **VP**

2

VP = Vanishing point

VP Horizon **VP**

3

Eye levels

If you go to the top of a building and look down, you are taking a *high eye level*. If you crouch at ground level you are taking a *low eye level*. When drawing from a high eye level, the horizon will be close to, or even right off, the top of your picture. If the view is seen from a low eye level the horizon will be near the bottom of your picture, and the tops of walls, houses and trees will stick up above it.

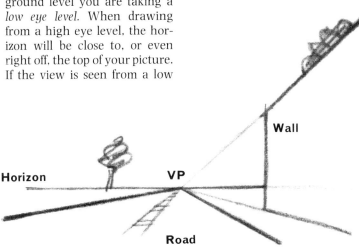

Low eye level

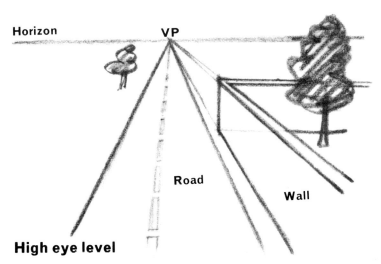

High eye level

29

Curves

A circle seen in perspective is more difficult to draw. The easiest way to do it is in two stages. First put the circle in a square. Then put the square into perspective. The circle becomes an oval, or an *ellipse*. The lower the eye level it is seen from, the more 'flattened' the circle is.

If you draw a *round* tower seen from a low eye level, the base of the tower will be part of a very flattened oval and the top will be part of a less flattened oval. If you want to draw it from a high eye level, you just reverse the ovals.

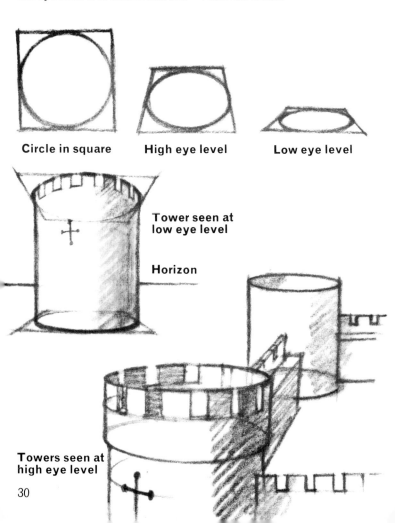

Circle in square　　**High eye level**　　**Low eye level**

Tower seen at low eye level

Horizon

Towers seen at high eye level

30

Scale

Large objects like castles show the effects of perspective very dramatically, especially when seen from close up. With small objects the perspective effect is much less dramatic. You can draw a match box life size, but not a castle! If you draw a castle, or any large object, to a small scale use perspective to help you to give an impression of its true size.

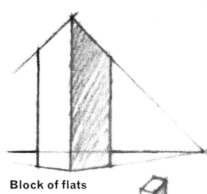

Block of flats

Matchbox

Foreshortening

A table top seen from above seems to occupy a greater area than when it is seen at an angle. When it is seen at an angle it is *foreshortened*.

Look at the drawing of the cube below. Which face is most foreshortened? Which is least foreshortened?

A cylindrical shape looks shorter, and the end appears more rounded, the more foreshortened it is. You can see this easily if you look at a few simple

Table top

Foreshortened

Cube

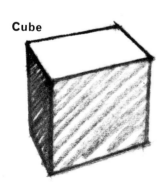

Very foreshortened!

cylindrical objects, like the cardboard tube from the middle of a used toilet roll, an old liquid detergent bottle, or even a pencil, as shown here.

Legs, arms and bodies can be thought of as cylinders, so once you have drawn a few foreshortened 'squeezy' bottles, you will find drawing things like horses and people much easier. Look at lots of solid objects in terms of foreshortened cylinders and cubes. Practise by

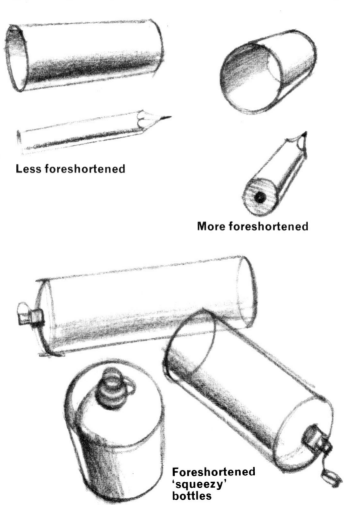

Less foreshortened

More foreshortened

Foreshortened 'squeezy' bottles

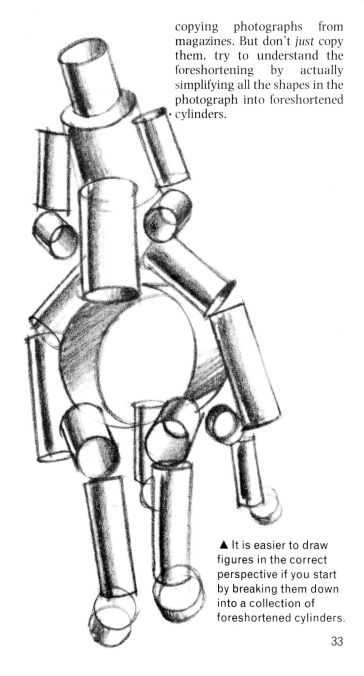

copying photographs from magazines. But don't *just* copy them, try to understand the foreshortening by actually simplifying all the shapes in the photograph into foreshortened cylinders.

▲ It is easier to draw figures in the correct perspective if you start by breaking them down into a collection of foreshortened cylinders.

33

When the foreshortening is right, work more realistic details into your drawing.

Practising perspective
Have fun drawing fantastic constructions, even if they look as if they might fall down! Make them simple tubes and blocks if you like, but try to get the perspective right.

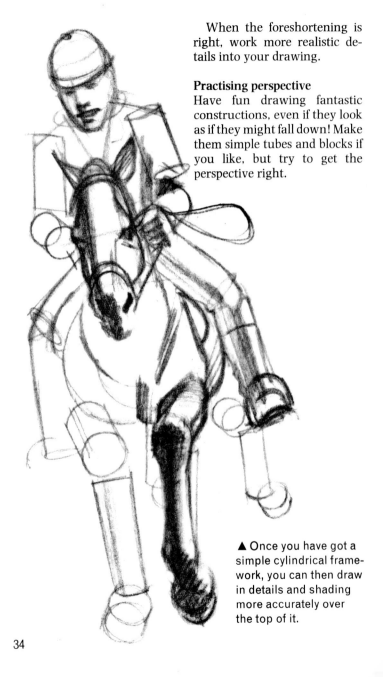

▲ Once you have got a simple cylindrical framework, you can then draw in details and shading more accurately over the top of it.

When you get used to thinking about where the vanishing points are and what your eye level is, it will be easier to draw convincingly. When you draw from life, always check the perspective of your drawing against the scene in front of you. Perspective is not just a mathematical formula. It is how you actually see!

▲ Draw your constructions large, like this. But use a big enough sheet of paper to include all your vanishing points.

4: Light and Shade

You can draw vanishing points onto your paper, but it isn't always so easy to get a light source onto paper – because the usual source of light is about 150 million kilometres away!

It *is* possible to put the Sun into your picture, of course, if you paint a sunrise or a sunset. Then other objects will be silhouetted against the light, throwing long shadows towards you, and the Sun will be the lightest thing in the picture (as shown below).

But usually the Sun will be out of your picture. The things you are drawing will not shine themselves, but simply *reflect* sunlight. When you start a drawing or a painting, first get it clear in your mind just where the light is coming from. Draw a little arrow in one corner, if you like, to remind yourself of its direction.

Direct and indirect light

Study the effects of light falling on a simple round object like a table tennis ball. The lightest part of the ball will be directly facing the source of light, but the darkest part is not necessarily on the opposite side from the light source.

The object you look at will not be isolated in space. It will be surrounded by other objects which might reflect light back onto it, lightening areas which would otherwise be dark. The

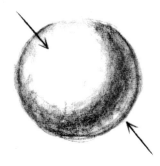

Direct light

Reflected light

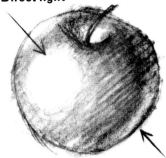

Direct light

Reflected light

Shadows and surfaces

Light and shade might be opposites, but you can't have one without the other! Since paper is white and pencil lead is dark, what you have to draw is the shadows around the white areas of light.

A shadow is related to the object which is throwing it. It is also related to the surface it is thrown *onto*, which might distort its shape. So as well as studying shadows, you should also study surfaces!

Surfaces, whether they are the ridges and furrows of the landscape or the hollows of someone's face, are usually fairly complicated. A way of

surface it is standing on may do this, for example.

When you think you understand the effects of light and shade on simple objects, try to relate what you have learned to more complicated shapes.

▲ Shadows falling onto an even surface.

▲ Shadows falling onto an uneven surface.

37

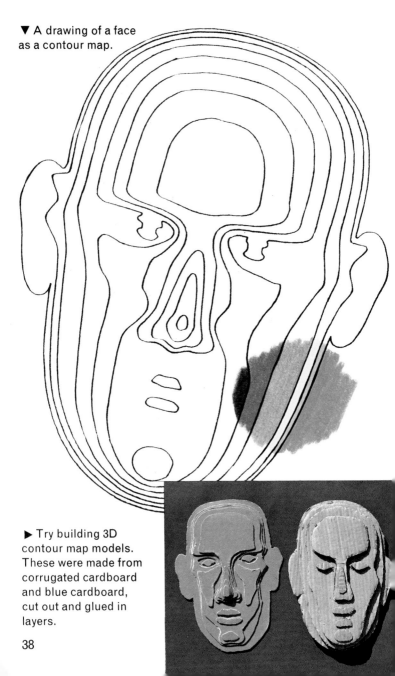

▼ A drawing of a face as a contour map.

▶ Try building 3D contour map models. These were made from corrugated cardboard and blue cardboard, cut out and glued in layers.

understanding complicated surfaces is to 'map' them.

If you look at a map of a mountain, the shape and height of it could be shown by *contour lines* (as if the mountain had been sliced through in layers from top to bottom). If you use contour lines to map a face, for example, you will avoid the temptation to only look at the obvious features like the eyes, nose and mouth. Other features, such as the cheek bones and the overall shape of the head, are just as important.

Face lit from above

Other light sources

The Sun is so far away that rays of sunlight falling on a scene are always parallel to each other. When a light source is close, its rays shoot out in all directions. Try drawing a firelit scene, with a low, central light source throwing huge shadows. Look in a mirror with your face lit from below to get the effect.

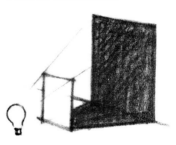

Close light source

Central light source

Face lit from beneath

5: Drawing Movement

It is always more difficult to draw subjects that don't keep still. So animal or human movement is a tricky subject to attempt.

Artists used to have to rely on direct observation, and with very rapid movement it isn't surprising that they usually got it wrong. Today, we have the advantage of photography, which can record every detail of the position of a moving body in a fraction of a second. So we can

▲ When a dog runs it repeats the same movements . . .

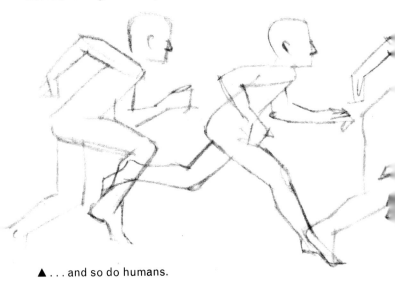

▲ . . . and so do humans.

study at length poses which, in life, might last for only a split second. It is also possible to study movie film frame by frame, so we haven't any excuse if we draw a horse with its legs moving in the wrong sequence (as artists always used to do).

It is very tempting to copy photographs and never look at the living subject at all. But if you observe from life, with the understanding to be gained from photographs, you get the best of both worlds.

Look first, draw later

It is a mistake to try to draw a moving object in the same way as a still life or a model holding a pose. It is better to spend at least twice as long looking at your subject as you do actually

drawing. When you want to draw something like an animal or a person running, spend *all* your time looking and save the drawing until later. Even if a pose only lasts for a split second, at least it is repeated again and again.

Most people make the mistake of wildly exaggerating a pose, and draw limbs flying in all directions. The beauty of movement is in its order and economy. Animals or athletes would never stay the course if they wasted energy.

The possible movement of each joint in a limb is limited, but two or three joints acting together add to the effectiveness of the movement. You may have to learn about animal

anatomy from books. But you can find out how human limbs work by trying out movements yourself before you draw them.

If you like to watch sport or dancing, look for the rhythms in movement. Remember and

▶ The drawing in the centre was copied from a photograph. On the left is an attempt to draw what the camera might have seen from a different angle. On the right is a pose the camera might have recorded a split second later.

then draw the typical poses that dancers and athletes adopt. Study photographs for the details it is so difficult to see in life. But don't just copy them, try to understand them too. To test your understanding, choose a photograph and try to draw the pose as it would have appeared if the camera had been in a different position. Or if the photographer had pressed the shutter release button a moment later.

6: Design and Composition

1   2

Whatever you plan to make – a power station, a pendant, or a painting – try out your idea in pencil first to check that it will work. In other words, make a design.

First, find out all you can about the materials you plan to use. If you are stuck for ideas go back to nature. Even quite abstract shapes can be derived from natural forms. A visit to a zoo, or even to a greengrocer's shop, may give you dozens of ideas. Even if you want to base your design on something as

▲ Stages in making a pendant.
(1) Sketch of a pillar box.
(2) Design based on the sketch.
(3) The finished pendant.

▼ A design should avoid having any thin pieces that may bend, cracking the enamel.

unnatural as a pillar box, go and look at one first.

A design problem

The design of a power station is very complicated, so let's look at pendants. The pendants shown here are made of enamelled copper. Copper bends easily. Enamel is glass, and you know what happens if you try to bend glass. These opposite qualities have to be made to work together in the design. The copper shape must be very compact, with no long, unsupported pieces which might bend, shattering the enamel. To make enamel, powdered glass is melted onto the copper in a kiln. It isn't easy to get fine details with powder, so the design must be simple.

▼ Compact shapes make a better base for enamelling.

People Alphabets

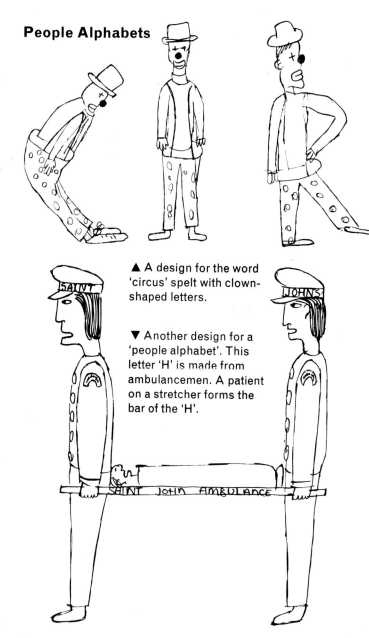

▲ A design for the word 'circus' spelt with clown-shaped letters.

▼ Another design for a 'people alphabet'. This letter 'H' is made from ambulancemen. A patient on a stretcher forms the bar of the 'H'.

With drawing and painting too, it is important to understand your materials. And to keep your design simple, by picking only the important details. The better you understand your subject the easier this is.

As an exercise, try designing an alphabet, but make it an alphabet with a difference – make the letters out of people! Combine groups of people to make up some of the letters. Use props, like the stretcher carried by these two ambulancemen. Or try to make the people fit the word they spell, like the clowns in the word 'circus'.

Illustration

Designing a picture is all about what to put in and what to leave out, and choosing the best angle. Illustrating a story is very good practice.

The drawings below illustrate William McGonagal's poem *The Tay Bridge Disaster* (look it up, it may surprise you). The poem tells the whole story, so the illustration can concentrate on dramatic details, like the terror of the train driver and passengers.

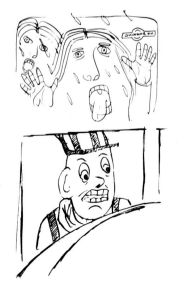

Composition

You should design a picture as carefully as you would design a piece of jewellery. Designing a picture is called *composition*. A composer of music arranges his rhythms and melodies to please the ear or to arouse the emotions. He doesn't simply try to copy natural sounds. This gives a clue about composing pictures.

You can't judge a painting by how much it looks like a photograph. However realistic it is, a painting isn't much good if the artist has failed to combine his colours, tones, **textures** and shapes cleverly, or to use his tools with skill.

The sheet of paper, board or canvas an artist works on is usually rectangular, because that is a more interesting shape than a square. If the picture is to be interesting too, there are a few rules of composition which are worth learning.

Tips to remember

AVOID lines which divide the picture into equal halves – whether it's vertically, horizontally or diagonally. Two-thirds to one-third is a better division and it is more effective to place the focus of interest away from the centre.

Pointed shapes direct the eye towards the next thing along, so DON'T have them pointing out of the picture. DON'T scatter points of interest evenly across the paper. Instead, group

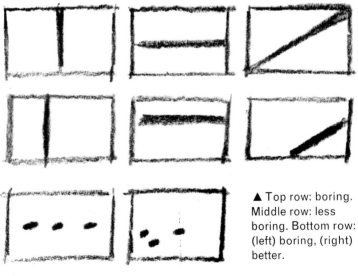

▲ Top row: boring. Middle row: less boring. Bottom row: (left) boring, (right) better.

48

◀ The central tree divides this composition vertically into two equal halves.

▶ The horizon divides the composition horizontally into two equal halves.

◀ The tree and the house are now too far apart. There is no focus of interest and the dark field directs the eye right out of the picture.

▶ Moving the tree to the right blocks the pointing effect of the field, and creates a focus of interest with the house.

them together to give the eye a definite place to look. It is worth remembering that most people will 'read' your composition from left to right, as they would with a book.

All this is fine when you are making up a picture, but how do you compose a picture when you are drawing or painting from life? If it is something small, like a portrait or a still

▲ The main subject here is the house.
It is seen framed by the gate, by the tree in
morning and in evening light, and by leaves of
the tree, made huge by the effects of perspective.

life, you can easily re-arrange the subject, light it differently, or try another viewpoint. If it is large, like a landscape, walk about in it. Find different angles and use perspective to make a small part, such as a tree or a bunch of leaves, fill much of your picture. You will have to let nature light it for you, but try to choose the weather and time of day which suits it best.

▲ Stonehenge, looking dramatic at sunset (30cm × 27cm). Colour patches are a quick way of checking your colours first.

Making a rough

If you are going to invest a lot of time and effort in a painting, it is worth making one or two *roughs* first.

A rough is a less detailed and usually smaller version of a painting you plan to make. The point of making a rough is to work out the composition, the colour scheme and so on. It is much easier to make changes and improvements on a rough than it is on your painting!

Even after you have begun the final version of your picture, it is not too late to make roughs. If you are not quite sure of a detail make a rough version on a separate sheet of paper to try it out, before you commit yourself on the actual painting.

◀ Trying out a detail.

▼ A first pencil rough for the painting on the right.

7: Abstract Art

My dictionary defines the meaning of the word abstract as 'to separate and consider apart', and 'a summary comprising the essence of'.

Whatever you draw or paint, you have to separate each part mentally, and decide whether to include it in the picture. You can never get *every* detail in, so all your pictures have to be summaries of the subject you are painting, or its *essence*.

But how do you decide what is essential? This is easier when you have a very clear aim, such as to design a 'people alphabet' (see pages 46–47), where you only need to select the features and poses that help to make the people look like letters. Or in drawing cartoons, like those on

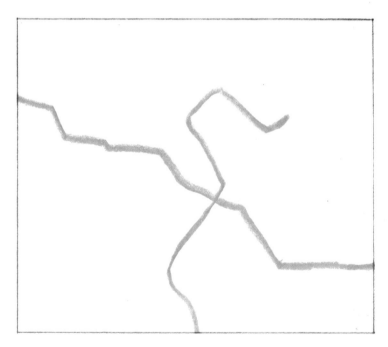

▲ Make a few random marks on paper.

pages 18–19. Here, you have to select and emphasize details like the big nose, which gives the face its character, or the wrinkles and large lower jaw of the bulldog.

Cartoons are one kind of abstract picture, but there is another kind in which the artist has no intention of making his picture look *like* anything. Instead he tries to put together lines, colours, tones and textures in an interesting way.

Practise this yourself by making a mark, such as a line or a coloured shape, on your paper. Then try to fill the paper with lines, shapes and colours which relate to your first mark. If you find it hard to get started, try using your initials as a basis for your picture.

Other abstract pictures *do* try to look like something. They try to look like a mood or a feeling! If the marks you make suggest a mood or remind you of an experience (going to the dentist, for example), use the shapes and colours to emphasize the mood you wish to create.

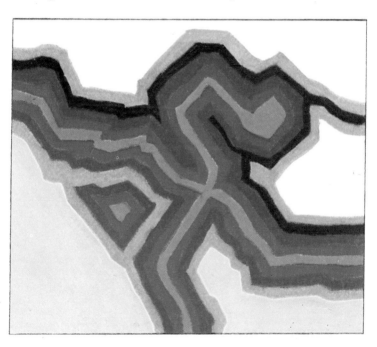

▲ Then build up other shapes and colours around them.

8: Colour

The colours we see are really different 'wavelengths' of light. You can see the full range of colours by separating white light through a glass prism. The result is a band of colours called a 'spectrum', with red light at one end and violet at the other.

Rain acts as a prism by splitting the light of the Sun in the same way, and turning it into a rainbow. The wavelengths of *visible* light are not the full picture, though. Beyond the red end of the spectrum, the wavelengths get longer and become heat, while at the blue end they get shorter and become ultraviolet, X-rays and gamma-rays.

Some creatures can see more

**Inside:
primary
colours**

**Outside:
secondary
colours**

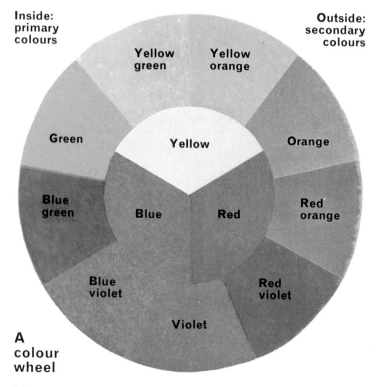

Yellow green

Yellow orange

Green

Yellow

Orange

Blue green

Blue

Red

Red orange

Blue violet

Red violet

Violet

**A
colour
wheel**

of the spectrum than we can. Insects can see ultra-violet light, for example, but what *we* call 'visible' light is all we have to worry about here.

Colour wheels

The range of colours in visible light can be shown as a colour wheel, with **primary colours** in the middle and **secondary colours** round the outside. Secondary colours can be made by mixing primary colours together in different proportions. Colours which are next to each other on the rim of the wheel *harmonize.* Colours which are opposite each other *contrast.*

You won't find black or white on the wheel, though. It is sometimes said that black and white are not actually colours at all. In terms of light this is true, because black is the absence of light and white is all the other colours mixed together. But it is not true of *pigments.* Pigment is what gives paint its colour, and if you mix all the different coloured pigments together you don't get white. You get mud!

Pigments

We see each type of pigment (or anything else) as a different colour because each one reflects a particular wavelength of light and absorbs the rest. Black pigment absorbs *all* the wavelengths of light. White pigment reflects them all. But the colours produced by pigments are rarely as pure as the colours of the spectrum. The colours found in paint are richer, more earthy colours; as you might

▲ Contrasting colours.

▼ Colours of the spectrum.

▲ Harmonizing colours.

expect from pigments which are dug from the earth or made from organic materials such as beetle's blood!

Pigments are now chemically purer and cover a wider colour range than ever before. But you often have to mix them to get the exact shade you want.

Mixing colours

Mixing colours is an art best learnt by trial and error. Try making your own colour wheel with more shades of colours around the rim. You have to have the three primary colours to start with, of course, so you can mix the secondary colours.

You can also mix all *three* primary colours together to make brown, or mix secondary colours in a variety of ways to make other shades not seen on the colour wheel. Or you can add black or white paint to make more varieties of each colour. White and red make pink, for example, and black and yellow make a different shade of green to that mixed from yellow and blue.

It is usually a mistake to try to lighten colours simply by adding white, or to darken them by adding black. It is better to look for less intense (or deeper) shades of the colour you are using, or to use cooler (bluer) colours to suggest shade, and warmer (more yellow) colours to suggest direct light. This is called *colour temperature*. Adding black or white to other colours, like mixing too many colours together, can make your painting look muddy and dull.

Colour schemes

When working out a colour scheme, try painting patches of colour on a spare bit of paper. Cut the patches up and try out different combinations. Sometimes the colours you least

▶ Use *colour temperature*, as well as light and dark tones, to suggest light and shade.

expect to work well work best!

Try out colours in the margin before committing yourself on the picture. (Sometimes the margins may end up looking more interesting than the painting!) If you do try this, you should then cut two large, L-shaped pieces of plain paper or card to mask over the margins. It is easier to judge how well the picture works with the margins and rough edges hidden. Try this with the sketch of Stonehenge on page 51.

▲ Cut up patches of colour to try out a colour scheme.

Practise some colour schemes. Scribble a few random criss-cross lines on paper, then fill in the shapes between the lines with different colours. Try several harmonizing colours and one contrasting colour.

▼ Two L-shaped pieces of paper or card, masking a colour scheme based on several harmonizing colours with one contrasting one.

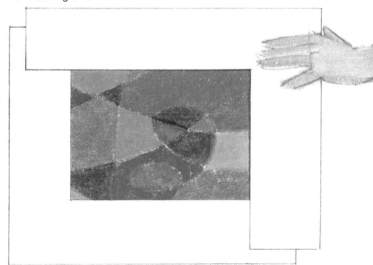

9: Choosing and Using Painting Materials

The most common mistake people make when painting is to start on the details before they have an accurate framework to relate the details to.

If you also find this hard to resist, use a bigger brush! Make a painting or two using only a small house-painting brush, so that you *have* to concentrate on broad shapes and colours instead of small details. Put in big, basic shapes with the full width of the brush. Any details that

▲ A picture painted with powder paint, using a small house-painting brush (26cm × 32cm).

Paints

	Water colour	Powder paints	Poster colour	Acrylic paints	Oil paints
Transparent	√	√		√	
Opaque		√	√	√	√
Paint onto: Paper	√	√	√	√	
Board	√	√	√	√	
Canvas				√	√
Canvas board				√	√
Hardboard				√	√
Walls		√		√	
Apply with: Brush	√	√	√	√	√
Fingers		√			
Palette knife				√	√
Solvent	Water	Water (Add PVA glue for murals)	Water	Water or Polymer Transparentizing medium*	Linseed oil or Turps**
Insoluble when dry	No	No	No	Yes	Yes

* This prevents the paint from drying too dull. It can also be used to 'varnish' your painting in order to revive colours which *have* dried dull.

** Buy varnish from an artists' supply shop to revive oils which have dried dull.

you think are *essential* can be put in by using just the corner of the brush.

Paints

All paints are a mixture of pigments (colours) and some sort of *medium* (glue) to hold the pigments in place. The medium can be gum, egg white, honey, linseed oil or emulsified plastic. Before the days of emulsified plastic, artists used to grind their own pigments and mix their own paints. Now paints come ready-made in convenient blocks, tubes or pots.

They also come in a bewildering range of colours. But you only need the primary colours to start with, plus black and white. Later on you can add other colours as you need them. But first you have to decide what *kind* of paint you want to use, as different kinds can't usually be mixed together.

Paints can be divided into those that are water-based and those that are oil-based. Or they can be divided into those which dry fast and those which don't, and so on. Each kind of paint has its own unique combination of qualities. Perhaps the most important difference is between paints which are *transparent* and those which are not. Paints which are not transparent are called *opaque*.

▼ A painting made with opaque poster paints. Inset is an enlarged detail of highlights.

If you use opaque paints, you can paint one colour over another without the first showing through, even if it is a *lighter* colour which you use on top. You can't do this with transparent paints. Transparent yellow painted over blue results in green. So does transparent blue painted over yellow! Even very light colours will affect darker colours painted on top.

Using water colour

Transparent paints are more difficult to use, since it is impossible to paint out your mistakes! The most transparent type of paint is water colour.

Water colours are, naturally, wet. If you make paper very wet it wrinkles as it dries, and who needs a picture with wrinkles? You can avoid this problem by painting on special water colour board, or by stretching your paper first.

To stretch paper you need a **drawing board**, some sticky brown paper tape and a wet sponge. Dampen the paper with the sponge, tear off four strips of tape and stick the paper (all round the edge) to the board. Squeeze out the sponge and dab off any surplus moisture, then let the paper dry out before painting on it. Don't remove it from the board until your painting is finished and dry, and it will stay flat.

▶ A painting made with transparent water colour paints. These three stages show how layers of darker and darker colours are built up.

Paint applied to the paper while it is still damp runs slightly on the surface, giving an attractive, soft appearance. It is possible to lift out sections with a clean brush or sponge, to make highlights or lighter areas such as clouds. Even after the paint is dry it is possible to soften and lift it out with a brush dipped in clean water. Water colours can be mixed in the lid of the paintbox or an old white saucer.

Using poster colour

Poster colour comes in tubes or pots and needs thinning with water before use. It should not be over-diluted or used as wet as water colour, so it isn't essential to stretch your paper. Colours can be mixed on any non-absorbent surface, such as a square of lino or an oil painting palette. For large amounts of colour, the faithful old white saucer comes in useful.

Because poster colours are opaque, you can simply paint over mistakes. But too much over-painting softens the layer of paint underneath. This mixes with and muddies the surface layer. So don't try to be too fussy and neat, but keep your brush strokes lively and free.

You can use thin poster paint, like water colour, to let the colour underneath show through, but this isn't easy.

Using powder paints

These come in tins as coloured powder. They should be mixed with water and can be used either transparent (thin) or opaque (thick).

If a little *PVA glue* is added to the mixture, the colours are

▲ The basic shape of this goldfish was first painted in dark blue poster paint, then overpainted in yellows and oranges used thin enough to let the colour underneath show through. This gave a darker cooler colour than the highlights, which were put in in opaque colours later (13cm wide).

▲ A mural painted in powder paint with PVA added.

richer and the paint will last longer. They cover large areas cheaply, which makes them useful for murals (see page 75).

Using acrylics

The medium used with acrylic paint is emulsified plastic, the same medium which binds emulsion paint on walls.

Like emulsion paint, acrylic mixes with water and is waterproof when dry. (So remember to wash your brush out right away!) If you mix the colours on an enamelled or china palette, you will be able to peel off old acrylic paint in a sheet before you start mixing more.

Acrylic dries very fast, so you can overpaint almost at once. It can be used either as a thin wash, like water colour, or thick, like oil paint. Used thick, it retains the ridges and brush strokes when dry, as oil paint does. You can also apply it with a **palette knife**, and you can mix in sand, bits of sacking, or anything that will give it texture.

Once set, the pigment and anything you mix with it, is enclosed for ever in a flexible plastic sheet! If you cover the surface with an acrylic **primer**, you can paint on paper, board, fibreboard, canvas board, canvas or walls.

Using oil paints

Oil paints are not cheap, and to use them you will have to invest in canvas or board and an easel. You don't *have* to paint in oils to be an artist, and it is worth trying your skill with something like poster paint first.

The medium which binds the pigment in oil paint is *linseed oil*. There is a certain amount already in the paint, but you need to add more. You can thin it further with *turpentine (turps) substitute*, which is highly inflammable. NEVER USE TURPS SUBSTITUTE NEAR AN OPEN FIRE AND ALWAYS KEEP THE TOP FIRMLY SCREWED ON THE BOTTLE.

A palette with a thumb hole is best for mixing colours. Squeeze out a little of each of the colours you need onto the palette. Have a little oil and turps ready in two small metal pots clipped to the side of the palette, called *dibbers*. Mix the colours in small amounts with the tip of a brush, or use a palette knife.

Some people like to use a palette knife to paint with too. Use the type that is shaped like a small trowel, with a thin, flexible tip, and the handle angled to clear the canvas. The paint used in this kind of work should be thicker than usual. Oil paint doesn't shrink when it dries, so the ridges left by the knife add life to the finished picture.

You can buy canvas board to work on, or prepared canvas mounted in a frame. Another useful material, which is cheaper to buy, is hardboard. You have to coat hardboard with a white primer before painting on it. Ordinary house paint primer is fine. You can use the smooth or the textured side of the board. It saves money to re-use oil paintings you don't want to keep. But paint them over with white primer first, so you won't be distracted by the old picture underneath.

▼ Detail of a palette knife painting.

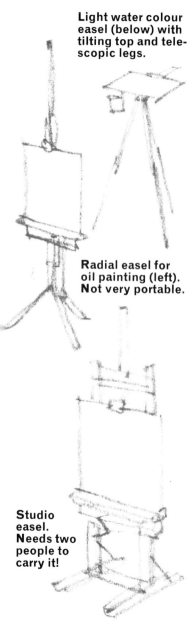

Light water colour easel (below) with tilting top and telescopic legs.

Radial easel for oil painting (left). Not very portable.

Studio easel. Needs two people to carry it!

Easels

Because oil paintings are usually large it is more important to have your picture upright while working on it. It makes it easier to step back to see the full effect of what you are doing. So you need an easel.

The old 'blackboard' type of easel isn't much use, especially outside in the wind. You need an easel with a horizontal bar at the top, held by a wing-nut, so that it can be moved down to grip your canvas or board. Have some newspaper and cloths handy to clean up with.

Brushes

Use a coarse, bristle brush for oils and acrylic and a finer brush for details. For other paints, use a brush made from nylon fibres or hair. The best brushes are made from sable hair, but even a brush made from a mixture of sable and some other kind of hair isn't cheap.

If you have invested in a good brush, look after it. Never force the hairs out at a sharp angle, or your brush will soon go bald. Always clean it carefully after use, in water for water-based paint, in turps for oils. Dry it on a cloth, gently squeezing it back into shape. DON'T leave brushes for too long in pots of water, unless you like your brushes to be banana-shaped!

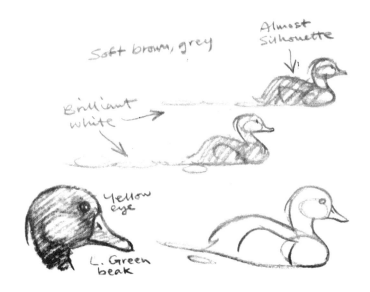

Soft brown, grey

Almost Silhouette

Brilliant white →

Yellow eye

L. Green beak

(1) The first stage in this oil painting was to make studies from life.

(2) The next stages were to cover the white background with a neutral colour and to sketch in the basic composition.

(3) The next stage was to establish the main darks and lights, then to try patches of colour to brighten the colour scheme.

(4) The finished painting (12cm × 16cm).

10: Drawing and Painting from Life

▲ Water colour of an otter (17cm × 21cm).

This picture of an otter was painted by a fifteen-year-old boy. It shows promise, but is based far too much on other artists' work and not enough on nature and a knowledge of the subject.

I know that because I painted it. Since then I have found that, while it is possible to learn a lot from other artists' work, nature is a far better model. When you want to paint something realistically, go and *look* at whatever it is you want to paint. Don't just look, either, but make some quick sketches and notes to take back with you. Then use them as a reference for more finished pictures, painted at home or at school.

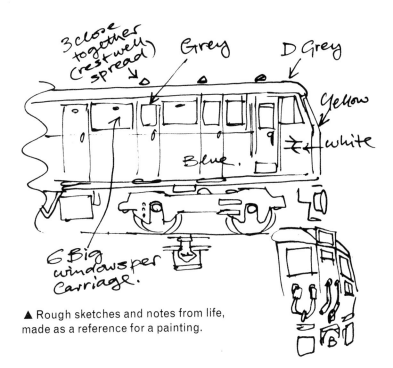

▲ Rough sketches and notes from life, made as a reference for a painting.

Studies

Sketches made as reference for a painting are called *studies*. But there is another meaning to the word 'study'. You study to learn, and you can make studies simply to learn about the subject you are drawing – to find out why it looks the way it does, how it works, how it appears in different positions, and so on.

You draw and paint best what you understand best. A sailor can usually draw a ship, even if he can't draw anything else. Artists have to try to understand *everything* they draw or paint. It helps to study your chosen subject in books, museums and elsewhere. But most of all, try to study it from life. Make dozens of drawings, from life if you can, from photographs in books if you can't. Illustrations in books often help to fill in details you may have missed in drawing from life.

Because these drawings are studies, they don't have to be finished. If your subject moves, or if you can see that your sketch is not accurate, start another drawing at once and

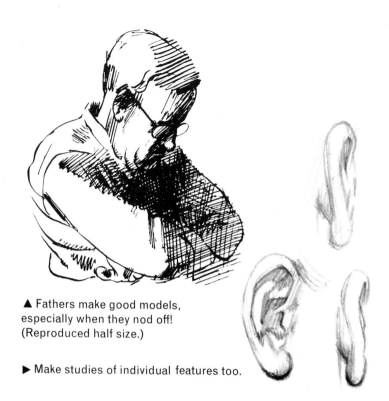

▲ Fathers make good models, especially when they nod off! (Reproduced half size.)

▶ Make studies of individual features too.

leave the first one unfinished. The object is not to produce a masterpiece, but to learn. The more you can find out about what you are drawing, the more convincing your drawing will be – even when you draw from memory, without references. There is always more to learn, so never give up making studies.

The best way to make finished paintings is to paint the whole thing from life. That often means working in the open air, however, which has problems of its own!

Drawing out of doors

You will need a stiff-backed **drawing block** and some bulldog grips when drawing out of doors. Or sheets of paper, a drawing board and some drawing pins. You need the bulldog grips to hold the loose end of the block closed, or the drawing pins to fix the sheets of paper to the board. Even on the calmest day, when you sit down to

▲ Uncles and aunts can usually be persuaded to pose for a few minutes. (Reproduced half size.)

draw, a force ten gale immediately springs up!

You will also need pencils or chalks, a small folding stool, and a thick skin! You need the folding stool because it is difficult to draw while standing and there isn't always a wall or log handy to sit on. You should be able to buy the right kind of folding stool quite cheaply from a camping shop.

You need a thick skin because people always seem to appear from nowhere to look over your shoulder while you are working!

Painting out of doors

You need just as thick a skin when you paint out of doors. An easel is also useful when you are using any type of paint except oils. With oils an easel isn't just useful, it's essential! But try a portable water colour easel, it's lighter to carry.

You need paints, brushes, water (or linseed oil and turps for oils), a pot for the water and

► Detail from a study of an antique car. The surfaces look hard and shiny. This is not due to any special painting technique, but because the shapes and colours are right. It pays to spend twice as long *looking* as drawing! (Reproduced half size.)

▼ Part of a page of pandas. These sketches were made as studies for a panda pendant (see page 45). (Reproduced half size.)

something to mix paints in. You need plenty of pieces of rag for cleaning palettes and brushes. If you are painting in oils you need some means of carrying your picture while it is wet (oils dry very slowly). Some oil paint boxes have clips in the lid to carry small paintings.

If you are planning to work on private property, it is essential to get permission. Warm clothes, coffee and sandwiches are also a good idea. Last, but not least, take your rubbish home with you – you might want to come back to the same place again!

11: Murals

Unlike dancers or musicians, we tend to think of a painter as a solo performer, but group painting can be fun.

Working as a group obviously only makes sense with large-scale work, such as *murals*. A mural is a picture painted directly onto a wall. But if everyone painted whatever they liked the result would be a mess. Just as an orchestra needs a conductor, a large group of painters needs a 'foreman' to direct their efforts.

A small group of three or four people *can* work well without a leader. But first they have to discuss the subject they want to paint, who will paint which sections of wall, and so on. It is a good idea to give everyone their own task. Each person is then responsible for seeing that their job gets done.

It is also a good idea to make a rough or two first. This needs accurate measuring and scaling down of the wall areas, and more discussion after the roughs have been made. Look for useful shapes in the walls themselves. A rainbow, for example, might fit beautifully round the curve of an arch.

An audience in a grandstand is a good subject for a gymnasium wall. Stairs just cry out to have people painted climbing them or sitting on them, and false windows or doors painted to trick the eye are fun. But you don't *have* to be clever. A landscape, tree or wizard's cave is fine, if that is what you want to paint.

BEFORE you start painting, wash the wall down – it's hard work painting on top of old grease and dirt. Roughly paint in the outlines of the whole mural before you bother with details. It is annoying to find that two peoples' sections don't fit together, when it is too late.

◀ Mural of *Captain Britain*.

Materials for murals

Powder paints can be bought in bulk, so they are ideal for painting large areas, AS LONG AS THEY ARE PROTECTED FROM RAIN! Mix small amounts of colour in old plates or metal foil food trays from supermarkets. For large quantities use buckets or washing up bowls, and paint with large, house-painting brushes or paint rollers.

Add a little PVA glue to the mixture to brighten the colours and make the paint longer lasting. You don't want your mural rubbing off on people's coats!

PVA glue isn't waterproof (though it can mess up your brushes if you let it dry before washing them out). So if you

▲ A mural of a tree, with artist.

▼ A group planning a mural try their ideas on paper first.

work outside you need another kind of paint. Ordinary emulsion is fine as long as it doesn't rain before it is dry. Oil-based paints (the kind you paint doors with) will last forever, but don't try to mix them with emulsion paint. Whichever paint you use, you can usually scrounge plenty of half-empty pots from parents or neighbours. If you are not sure of a paint, try a small patch on the wall and let it dry, in case it comes out the wrong colour, or flakes off.

The soft effect of sprayed paint can look good in murals, but if you need to spray a hard edge, stencils can be cut from newspaper and stuck down at the edges with masking tape.

▲ Wizard's cave mural.

▼ Making the shapes of the mural fit the architecture.

77

Glossary

Depth The relative lightness or richness of shading or a colour.

Drawing block Sheets of paper arranged for drawing on a stiff backing board, bound along one side like a book or pad.

Drawing board A flat, rigid surface, usually of wood, to which paper can be pinned or clipped.

Framework The basis of a drawing or painting; the first guidelines drawn for a picture.

Highlight The brightest light reflected from an object; the white or light paint, or area, applied to a picture to suggest this.

Horizontal In line with the horizon.

Intermediate Between one thing and another, as greys are intermediate between black and white.

Opaque paints Paints with which one colour will cover another completely. Not transparent.

Palette A surface on which paints can be mixed. Some palettes have a thumb hole so they can be easily held while working.

Palette knife A knife with a flexible, unsharpened blade for mixing oil or acrylic paints.

Parallel lines Lines the same distance apart throughout their length, like railway lines.

Primary colours Colours from which all other colours can be mixed. They are yellow, red and blue.

Primer A first coat, or undercoat, which seals a surface. Without primer some surfaces will absorb the oil from oil paint, making it look dull.

Secondary colours Colours which can be mixed from the primary colours.

Shades Different tints or tones of a colour.

Shading Areas drawn or painted to suggest the darker parts of an object, or the section of it which is in shadow.

Structure The way things are put together, the essential framework of things.

Texture The roughness or *grain* of a surface; for example, the woven surface of a fabric.

Vertical Upright.

Index

Acknowledgements

The author would like to thank Blandford Books for allowing him to reproduce here the two illustrations on pages 18–19 from his book *Drawing Cartoons*; Tana Meinertzhagen for allowing him to use her beautiful charcoal drawings as illustrations in this book; Graham Sergeant for putting his camera at the disposal of the author; Mrs Morgan, headmistress of Horizon School, for giving him permission to use his slides of the murals in her school; and the pupils of Horizon School, Hackney Downs School and Bishop's Stopford School for teaching him so much.